THE PORTAGE POETRY SERIES

SERIES TITLES

Bone Country
Linda Nemec Foster

Not Just the Fire
R.B. Simon

Monarch
Heather Bourbeau

The Walk to Cefalù
Lynne Viti

The Found Object Imagines a Life: New and Selected Poems
Mary Catherine Harper

Naming the Ghost
Emily Hockaday

Mourning
Dokubo Melford Goodhead

Messengers of the Gods: New and Selected Poems
Kathryn Gahl

After the 8-Ball
Colleen Alles

Careful Cartography
Devon Bohm

Broken On the Wheel
Barbara Costas-Biggs

Sparks and Disperses
Cathleen Cohen

Holding My Selves Together: New and Selected Poems
Margaret Rozga

Lost and Found Departments
Heather Dubrow

Marginal Notes
Alfonso Brezmes

The Almost-Children
Cassondra Windwalker

Meditations of a Beast
Kristine Ong Muslim

Mouth

Thank goodness that Amorak Huey understands our craving for skillful poems that are unafraid to be both sweet and rude. We need the mega-poem called "Bodies, in Concert," the bawdy aubades, the lines that admit: "our greatest fear is morning comes / our greatest fear is mourning comes." Threaded among the ironic odes and the concerns of mid-life commitments are quick, piercing considerations of mortality and ecological peril. The voice of *Mouth* is confident in its moves, sometimes breath-stopping in its leaps, by turns despairing and lusty, deeply funny, and—always—restoratively human.

—SANDRA BEASLEY
author of *Made to Explode: Poems*

Amorak Huey's *Mouth* is an exploration—sometimes gentle, sometimes raucous—of one of the fundamental forces of nature: desire. In its quiet corners and its echoing sweeps, this collection returns to us our creatureliness and our (futile? noble?) attempts to transcend it, reminding us that our bodies were born "to crave / and end." Meanwhile, the planet burns. Meanwhile, all around us are the loves of our lives: people and music and landscapes and memories and new beginnings and "our dry lakebeds, / our impetuous affairs." *Mouth* can hold them all and, indeed, holds them out to us in a beautiful and tender rendering of both our absurdity and our magnificence. If we must crave and end, and if we must do it in this particular moment of human and geologic time—and, of course, we must—how lucky we are to have *Mouth* as our companion.

—MOLLY SPENCER
author of *Invitatory*

If it is possible to make a guitar amp for the soul, to hear what moon, river, barn, and paramour all desire of each other, Amorak Huey has done it in *Mouth*. Each line is electric, illuminating poems that extend their metaphors, believing to endure in language is to make love endure. Huey leverages, as all evocative poets do, the ways the body's intuition is always two steps ahead of the mind's reflexive need for order. With high fidelity to the philosopher's discursive insight, the concert goer's raw enthusiasm, and the naturalist's tenderness, this collection sings us a bridge toward the chorus of our collective hearts. Truly, he reminds us how, "It's the listening body / that's fresh. We cannot hear / with the same ears twice."

—STEVEN LEYVA
author of *The Opposite of Cruelty*

MOUTH

poems

Amorak Huey

CORNERSTONE PRESS
UNIVERSITY OF WISCONSIN-STEVENS POINT

Cornerstone Press, Stevens Point, Wisconsin 54481
Copyright © 2026 Amorak Huey
www.uwsp.edu/cornerstone

Printed in the United States of America.

Library of Congress Control Number: 2026931107
ISBN: 978-1-968148-28-7

Cornerstone Press titles are produced in courses and internships offered by the Department of English at the University of Wisconsin–Stevens Point.

DIRECTOR & PUBLISHER
Dr. Ross K. Tangedal

EXECUTIVE EDITORS
Jeff Snowbarger, Freesia McKee

EDITORIAL DIRECTOR
Brett Hill

SENIOR EDITORS
Paige Biever, Reilly Crous

PRESS STAFF
Lilly Kulbeck, Allison Lange, Sophie McPherson, Sam Bjork, Madison Schultz, Autumn Vine

For the rivers and the moon—
who else?

ALSO BY AMORAK HUEY:

POETRY

Dad Jokes from Late in the Patriarchy

Boom Box

Seducing the Asparagus Queen

Ha Ha Ha Thump

TEXTBOOK

Poetry: A Writer's Guide and Anthology (w/ W. Todd Kaneko)

CONTENTS

"All the labor of man is for his mouth,
and yet the appetite is not filled."
                                —*Ecclesiastes*

Self-Portrait as Ode to the Moon (the moon is an unreliable narrator) (the river too)

Forgive me. I no longer have time for your cold beauty,
moon,

your air of chill & mystery, your knowing
my secrets,

your power to slosh the oceans side to side
like the beer that's one too many at the dwindling of the block party

skateboarding around the rim of a red plastic cup
in the unsteady grip of someone with their eyes

on someone else,
but you, moon,

your unblinking gaze unlines me.
Early skygazers mistook your dry plains

for seas, moon,
so I expect you're accustomed to our poor judgment,

our many dry lakebeds,
our impetuous affairs,

but I am tired of hiding my desire from you, moon,
& you, too, river,

get over yourself
with your beautiful cascades,

something something sound of water over rocks,
your boasts about never making the same mistake twice.

The bees? The bees can stay.

Irreconcilable (ars poetica) (love poem)

When the world is settled & things in their place,

indeed this is the reason to go to the lake.

When we go to the lake & paint, there is no world,

we will go the lake & paint in peace.

Ode to the Seediest Motel in Kentucky

We find each other here, down the hill from an abandoned mall —
so much space we no longer use.

We have never felt more American.
But we could make this work.

A rootless life.
Dirty carpet & the song of passing traffic.

What if there were no one waiting anywhere?
No home

but hope?
No highway

out of these bodies,
no checkout time,

no exit
but the end of the world?

Ode to Temptation

I feel like I read somewhere that the fruit from the tree of knowledge was not an apple as commonly thought but a plum. We had plum trees & apple trees in our garden when I was growing up. The plums were small & the apples were sour. I kept a spoon from the kitchen under the T-shirts in my dresser & used it to sneak bites of brown sugar from the yellow box in the pantry. Was it the sweet I craved or the stealing? Did I learn then to associate my favorite flavor with the forbidden, the illicit, the under-cover-of-dark? Is it why I now enjoy being alone in my house? Does it explain the nonsense I believe about love? Or hunger? When I say I don't believe in original sin, am I forgetting that saccharine crumble dissolving on my tongue? ANYWAY what I'm saying is that Eve was right, when someone offers a taste you take it no matter the cost.

Bodies, in Concert

After all these years you're still chalking lines
around our love life, you're changing
positions to whatever's efficient. You run
your fingers across my throat, you pinch
& grant permission. *Finish*, you say,
& I do. God, that word in your mouth
gets me hot, bothered, done. Is it the word
or is it your mouth? Yes, I'm as easy
as I was at nineteen, I listen
to mostly the same music, adore
the same predictable rhymes: lips,
hips, fingertips, girl, world, love
& glove & the metal of desire
like a battery on my tongue. Positive
to positive, negative to ground,
turn the key & hope for the best,
sometimes the car turns over, sometimes
a problem is too big to jump-start.
I drove an '81 Civic, a shoebox
on wheels with fuzzy seat covers.
Did you ever do it on fuzzy seat covers?
a girl once asked & I died
& tried to pull off a *maybe*,
managed only the kind of coy
that says obviously not.
I cared so much about the size
of my speakers. I pretended to know
the best pattern for my equalizer.
If you max out everything it's just volume,
a girl once said. *I know*, I said,
as if I knew anything. I said yes
to everything then, as now, or would have
had anyone been offering. I saw

Guns 'n Roses in the muddy infield
of a horse track. They were late to the stage
& bored, playing songs
from an album no one had heard.
Someone threw a thick handful of mud
at Axl during "Patience," fouling
his white leather pants
so he stomped off-stage. The band
kept playing, unsurprised —
a lesson about what we can learn
to work around, perhaps, or what we sacrifice
to get what we want. Touch me
with the lights out & I'll melt down
all my rings for you. If there's a chance
you'll come back I'll never stop
strumming. Skid Row opened that concert
& the drummer flashed us his genitals,
we went wild, because whatever,
we were in love with the idea
that there might be no rules.
Someone also threw something at the stage
the night I saw Cinderella; the guitarist
caught it & threw it back — a beer cup,
I think — said, *Don't throw your shit at me*,
& we went wild, because whatever.
God, it was glorious to be alive
those days. When I look back & try
to figure out why, my best guess is
that it felt like spring all the time because we
were so startlingly wrong about the future.
Every song was a promise —
when you know nothing about sex
"smooth up in ya" sounds like every dream
you've ever had. I should be embarrassed
by the banality of my desires, nothing

original about being another hungry boy
in a world full of them, thinking
this music was written for us,
about us, the fortunes being told
ours. I saw Poison open
for David Lee Roth. I saw Winger
& Firehouse & Warrant. Look,
I never said I had taste. I never said
I could tell the difference
between music & noise,
between desire & hunger. "Cherry Pie"
is a fine metaphor, give me a break,
I like what I like. I never
said I would make a good husband,
or lover, but I am pretty sure
no one will ever want you more
which I mean not as a judgment
of your desirability
but of the boundlessness
of my desire. I saw Mötley Crüe,
umlauts & all, in Birmingham
with some friends who spun
their car into a ditch on the drive
to the concert. They started the show
with "Kickstart My Heart,"
all motorcycle rev & potential,
here there will be mayhem,
at some point Tommy Lee mooned us,
all bare-ass & dare-you audacity,
we went wild because obviously.
I told you it felt like a promise.
My friends threw their liquor bottles
in the woods before the cops arrived,
got a tow to the civic center,
made it in time, called their parents

later with some invented story
about bad luck. We were so young.
Immortal. The kind of young
that sets its own house on fire
to prove no flame can touch it.
We invented music. We invented
language for what we craved. It dawned
on us only later how inevitable
it all was. Or did it? Maybe
we're as clueless as ever,
still imagining ourselves as the first
to set foot on this strange planet —
trepidatious at first, one shaky foot
in front of the other in the darkness
& dust, into more darkness,
more dust — how did I end up here?
I thought this was about music.
Thought it was about marriage.
Thought it was about lust.
Now I'm stranded in a moon
orbiting around your body
reaching for you in hope,
the path familiar, the pattern
repeating like a chorus. When it's done
well it sounds new at each iteration.
I used to think it was something
in the song that'd changed
but no. It's the listening body
that's fresh. We cannot hear
with the same ears twice. We
cannot touch with the same fingers,
cannot be touched in the same flesh.
We are rivers. We are the stone
under the rivers. We are the stone
in the cherry — a surprise,

all that sweetness against lip & tongue,
& then resistance. Danger
if we bite too recklessly. The possibility
that a tree might grow if only
we took the time to plant
what we've been given. I told you
it was a perfectly fine metaphor,
far more pleasing than the half-ass narrative
of "Uncle Tom's Cabin." *Someone* knows
what happened to the bodies.
What happens to all bodies.
I keep losing focus. Losing track
of what matters. The night before
the Warrant concert, I went with friends
to see the band play softball
against local DJs at a downtown park.
Is there a dumber way to spend a summer evening?
I can't think of what it might be.
Yet three decades later
I remember how that evening felt —
like I was close to something important.
To something that mattered,
although nothing has ever mattered less.
That proximity — chasing nearness.
That's what I remember.
More than the songs, which were dumb
but fine. More than the friends
I was with, some of whom remain friends.
No offense to any of them. But what
I remember is the gap between my body
& the music. The gap between
my body & yours & the anything
I would give to bridge it. Now
I'm talking about last night
& the night before & that night

a few months ago after all those beers
that had us laughing at the bar
down the street from this life
we've assembled from a box of assorted parts
like an IKEA dresser. *Finish*,
& I do, not always as quickly as you'd like
& sometimes quicker. We keep
the instructions as if we might need
them again someday. As if we would
be able to find them if that day
ever came. I saw Lynyrd Skynyrd
at the state fairgrounds with my parents
when I was too young to care.
I saw Bon Jovi on the Slippery When Wet tour
when I thought "You Give
Love a Bad Name" was the best song
in the history of songs. Later
I thought that about "Pour Some Sugar on Me."
Maybe I still do. Maybe I have a taste
for sweetness. I'm equivocating here —
obviously, I do have such a taste. We reveal so much
about ourselves by what we hesitate
to admit. Which fires we set
& which ones we extinguish.
Which planets we orbit, which we avoid.
Someone asked what we were going to do next
& I said I thought we had time
for at least one more adventure
after this next one. You said you hadn't
thought of it that way. I said
once we've pulled up these roots
we can do anything.
You said okay. I swooned.
I held out my hand in hope.
It feels like a betrayal to say nothing

happened next, but nothing
happened next. It's like that sometimes.
We can't always be in the same mood.
Axl left the stage, but he came back
& finished the show.
He sounded terrible, is how
I remember it, but he finished
& maybe said *Good fuckin' night, Birmingham*
after "Paradise City," & we went home
pissed & covered in mud.
I left my shoes on the front porch
& threw them away a few days later,
& Guns 'n Roses' next concert
ended in a riot somewhere in the Midwest
so we were lucky, I guess. Could
have been worse. Could always be worse.
Sometimes you don't get what you want,
sometimes you do & it's worse.
Imagine making a hit song you don't like
& having to play it every night
for the rest of your life. Sure,
you'd be making all those people happy
but how many times can you sing
the same stupid rhyme
before you lose your mind?
How many ways to say please,
how many excuses can you make
for your body's clumsiness?
It's keeping you alive, for now,
what else can you ask. The mistake
is thinking time moves only forward,
thinking the order on the album
is the only order. Thinking love
is inevitable. Thinking love
means touch, happily means

ever after when all it means is now.
There's a reason many albums
open with the hit, a reason most hits
are three minutes. I saw Trixter
when the only song I knew
was their hit. I saw Wilson Phillips
because a girl put her fingers in my mouth
& asked, "Hold On" on repeat
on her cassette deck. I don't remember
the concert. It doesn't matter.
I remember the girl. Her fingers.
You're out of town tonight
& I'm half-watching a bad movie.
The body remembers, the leading man says.
Stores it up inside. He's talking about violence
but it could be music. Could be us.
You & me. The way you're miles from here
& if I close my eyes I can feel
your hands on me. Your skin
under my hands. You're in a cabin
by a lake. A hotel in a new city.
An apartment in a new life.
Reading poems in a bathtub.
Someone else's bed, or not,
doesn't matter, it's your body.
What movie are you half-watching?
When you close your eyes
what song comes to mind?
Can you feel my fingers?
When I saw .38 Special
we left early because my friend
who drove us had a football curfew
& we didn't much care
about the band anyway,
it was something to do.

When I said earlier I still listen
to the same music, I didn't mean
only the same music. When I said
I want, I didn't mean only want.
Except, you know, I did mean that.
Every song is about the same thing —
the songwriter's body taking flight
in search of love. Hairspray
& leather pants & stagecraft
doesn't change what's underneath,
I mean, we walk into the world every day
& put on a show. Sometimes
people leave early. Sometimes
we're bored & it's obvious. I'm
talking about all of it now. That's
how language works, words
always mean every possible thing,
you have to be careful. How far
have we come from where we started?
Look, it's how things go,
the inevitable path of the human experience,
we decide on a direction & set out
& sometimes we get lucky.
Sometimes we have someone to hold
hands with along the way, or someone
waiting at the end of the day
when we come home covered in dust or mud —
someone to shower with
& take to bed. How a song ends
has changed over the years,
they used to fade out
as if the music hadn't ended at all,
was still playing somewhere
& it was us who'd moved on,
already singing the next song

even as the first one continued
in some other room, a lover
moving on with their life as we
moved on with ours. When
Def Leppard's drummer lost his arm
in a car accident, it took a while
for us to hear what happened,
news spread differently in those days,
so by the time we knew the story for sure,
the band had resumed performing
& Rick Allen had an electronic kit
he could play with his feet. None of this
is metaphor, it's what happened
in the world. Not everything
stands for something else. Some
things simply are. Like us. We are.
We exist in this world as a lesson
to no one, about nothing,
not cautionary tale or exemplar,
not fable or psalm, sermon
or poem. One body & another body,
side by side in bed at the end of a day,
at the end of the next day, & the next,
until the bodies expect each other's
presence. The absence of absence.
This is what we wanted. What
we've always wanted,
though we probably would not have said so,
not back then, not before.
I saw KISS in concert long after their prime,
after the makeup had come off
leaving only the band,
unadorned & trying too hard,
& music that never quite sounded
the way it once had. It sounds

like a metaphor but it's life
which I guess makes it a metaphor.
I saw Living Colour early
& Slaughter late, Vixen even later.
We had no idea, back then,
so many of these bands
would be touring for decades.
I guess we should have known
when we saw the Stones
& they were our parents' age
& every note sounded like nostalgia.
Still, good show. They were all good shows,
even the ones we didn't like.
Good enough, at least. Music
& anticipation can get you through
most days. Before a concert
there's a moment when everyone decides
it's time to get closer to the stage,
there's a swell of noise,
a rush, a gathering. There's no signal,
nothing happens, but someone
moves, then someone else,
& then everyone in the general admission
area crushes together. This happens
too soon, always. The show is not
about to begin. From the stage
a roadie or guitar tech looks up,
smiles, waves. The crowd goes wild
because, whatever, it's better
than nothing, everyone's
in on the joke, let him enjoy pretending
he's the reason they're here, & besides
the proximity is a gift. All those bodies,
the heat they create, why
be in such a hurry. Finish? No,

we're just getting started. I don't mean
to make light of any of this. I don't mean
for it to make sense. After all these years
we're only bodies in the dark,
outlined in chalk, or not
yet. I mean all of us, everyone,
but also I mean you & me,
specifically, here, right now, this very moment,
in this hour, in this lifetime,
at the end of this path,
warm & so very alive,
hearts beating time, skin electrified,
waiting for the music to begin,
waiting for one of us to reach for the other.
Ask me anything. The answer is yes.

For So Long, I Was Foolishly Proud of The Scar on My Thumb

I wanted to be a man
until I met enough men

to know better. The pain
of understanding that arrives too late

is the teeth of handsaw
against skin, a mistake

while dragging away limbs
after a storm; I rend

my flesh like wax,
a wound that's worse

when I look at it. My own blood,
the white of my bone

exposed. Bleached, dying
coral. Ashed-over desert,

one dry lakebed
after another. I thought

I was helping. I thought
I was restoring order. I have

no excuse for the damage
I have done. Men are killing

the world. My skin will heal.
Will knit a pale contrail

across the smaller sky of my body.
Will still be the skin of a man.

The Phrase Is "Comfortable in Your Own Skin" but Who Has Ever Felt Such a Thing?

goddamn everything seems so important & so futile

apparently I need a new measles shot
often we think we've eradicated a kind of harm
it returns & it's always worse

hey did you also wake blinking in darkness
breathing hopefully until you remembered
which timeline this was

which of our bodies' promises
broken & when

anyway there's more wind than usual this spring

I Am So Thirsty to Be Wanted That

I invent someone
in a dream about kissing
then put them in a poem
kissing me

then because I am
happily married
in my waking life
pretend the poem

is invented
hypothetical
someone else
kissing someone else

on the banks of a river
I used to swim in
the river was
a long time ago

but the dream
the dream
was last night
the thirst ongoing

You Told Me Always to Add "In Bed" to the End of My Fortune Cookie Fortunes. I Told You the Same Thing Works on Poems but I Was Just Trying to Impress You. In Bed.

the dark breaks against your body
your skin reflects light from somewhere
or is it the silver of your whole self I see
when did you become the moon
this not how we planned any of this
we are supposed to be touching
are we supposed to be touching
my fingers at the edge of you
your body at the broken edges of my body
your mouth the clock we measure our hours by
your moan my moan one throat together
your water my water the water we spill together
time the only promise we cannot break together
we cannot go to sleep
our greatest fear is morning comes
our greatest fear is mourning comes
still so much touching left undone

We Wake Each Day in This World We've Made Together

The first thing I notice about this world is its mouth.
Its many mouths.

The way each opens differently,
angle of teeth or tongue held

just so — all the ways
to be consumed.

All the caverns
in the surface of this place,

their depths,
their dripping darknesses.

Simply to be alive
here is to be

at risk.
I'm talking

of course
about

the planet of being in love with you,
the hungriest planet,

this world we've made together,
the aesthetics of it —

the body of it.
All mouth. All plunder.

Dryer the Ground, More Dangerous the Floods

we knew there'd be a cost
we thought ourselves prepared to pay

we embraced then braced
to sleep & say goodbye

stay dry stay dry
in all this rain

& yet we wake
already wet as waters rise

someone watching would see it in our eyes
such surprise

to find that flood is punishment after all
still! we have nothing to repent

not the desire nor the dream
we thought gone meant clean

it's the other way around
the washing then the washing away

Ode to My Stupid Mouth

My mouth has no idea we're in a pandemic.
My mouth cannot stop dreaming about sex.
My mouth's fatal flaw is hunger. My mouth
is the maple limb that storm-splintered
into the backyard overnight, wrecking nothing.
It is a sidewalk splattered with wet forsythia petals,
sticky & fading. It is the lightning,
the thunder, the drench. My mouth is not the same age
as the rest of my body. The rest of my body
is a paper sack of bleached flour —
it cannot be refolded neatly, cannot stop spilling.
My mouth is a map of all my desire, is the red circle
around the towns I have lived in,
is beauty mark & mole, bite & scar
& bitter grudge. It remembers everything.
My mouth is a country that cannot stop
hurting its citizens. My mouth is ghost,
monster, dinosaur. The rest of my body
curls into quarantine but my mouth is outside
looking for someone to kiss. My mouth
will promise anything you ask,
go anywhere you want it to. My mouth
is responsible for every lie I've ever told,
my mouth wants to confess & be forgiven
as if that is love: tonguing language
into the world in hopes it comes back changed.

Sin

Hand lifted to mouth —
our first gesture —

how else to stave off this hunger?
How else the blackberry's sweet stain?

What the Moon Sees in Us

The moon can't believe we walk around
as if our hearts aren't broken.

We raise our eyes to the sky
as if the sky has something

to offer besides our shared secrets
rising like mist from the graveyard

of the distance between us,
the silence we still call love.

Besides, you know I'm going
to bring up your mouth again,

my desire, the ghost
of your kiss. I can summon

my disappointments at will
or they can summon me.

What Happens When a Star Explodes

It's like this, right. It's like when there's a moment moving furniture, right, something your arms cannot contain, your fingers cannot dig into, something impossibly heavy, a dining table perhaps, a sleeper sofa whose convenience you once thought outweighed its weight but that's true only when you're *not* standing at the top of a steep flight of stairs losing the battle against gravity, your muscles tense & quivering & giving way, there's this moment, right, when your body knows you've already lost but the end hasn't happened yet & in that moment all the weight goes away, the world goes away, leaving nothing, but there is light, only light, light, lightness, & then, only then, the fall.

I Have Been Taking Photographs of Dandelions

My hands flex & twitch
in the shape of far-away you;

my mouth dreams of your mouth.
What haunts this sleeping animal?

What blossoms in this foolish
time zone between us?

We once measured
together in hours,

apart in heartbeats —
wishes sent wild on the wind.

Light Years (marriage)

Telescope into Michigan   light from 23 years ago
        pink copper sunset smear above highway

Telescope   we see only   what is behind

Telescope   time machine

Telescope so deep into space
        pillars of creation   this ember

billow of dust   a star someday

billions of   Telescopes   of years

Telescope we came here seeking future
        found past

Telescope & other lies   it's always easy
        always hard   it's always

Telescope we have no analog for the images
        hole   Eye of Sauron   open woodstove

depth of winter Telescope
        pray for warmth   pray

the house does not burn   Telescope
        promises
the house will burn   has burned   all houses burn

Solstice

I imagine the darkened room
in which you awaken to wonder

where I am. I have not gone far,
my love. I picture you: still but alert,

arms crossed over your body
as if cradling someone,

eyes reflecting light from somewhere,
grey or green or the pale color

of a flipping coin. Our story, a toss-up;
could have gone either way,

a word spoken instead of swallowed,
a whisper warm against an ear

& I feel the season changing beneath me,
like the sea catching its breath

& reversing direction, slowly,
swelling against still-damp sand,

returning to cover what it so recently left behind.
Have you closed your eyes

to slip back into some almost-familiar dream?
Do your lips taste of salt?

Summertown

So armpit-hot our sidewalks sweat. Children melt. The dying river plunks nickels into a pay-by-the-minute window unit in the Afternoon Hotel where citizens meet spouses not their own. The water oaks lean precariously against each other as the ground turns to chalk around their roots. One old friend betrays another's trust when it would have been so easy not to. A group of women sit on the courthouse steps to drink gin over melting ice. It is as if they have been here all along. They have protest signs but the words are faded to nothing. The air smells of melted tar. It's easy to imagine dinosaurs sinking in, leaving only bones.

Love Poem

My body does not have a sophisticated relationship

with hunger. More,
the mouth says. More.

I Have Been Trying to Make Sense of Love Again

I thought to compare us to the weather
but rain never lasts.

I read somewhere
a cloud weighs millions of pounds —

no wonder, then,
the cloud eventually cannot hold.
& so, rain.

We are always in such a hurry to find shelter.
I want to hold still
in the wet

long enough to take a picture —
a way to remember us that way

or a failsafe against the inevitable forgetting.
Perhaps I've missed the point.

Perhaps I was thinking of the moon.

Do Not Be Hasty in the Laying on of Hands, Do Not Share in the Sins of Others, & Other Terrible Advice

I have no way to remember how your palms feel
against my face
or anywhere

but I imagine the music we'd listen to
Grace Potter maybe

or Brandi Carlisle
smart & sultry like that & I imagine

the exact dimness

a hotel room say
bathroom light left on
accidentally

but the moment for turning it off has passed

so now there's the music & just enough light

keep your eyes open you say
slow you say

when hunger & stillness fight who wins

Ode to Late Summer

I hear the neighbors laughing with friends on their back porch
& I'm thinking about sex
a couple might have
after an evening of company.
Tired sex. Eyes-closed sex. Grateful sex,
the-dishes-are-done sex,
just-the-two-of-us-at-last sex
that-Indigo-Girls-song-we-like-on-low sex.
It's been so hot, but today was clouds & cool,
a front moving in from the west.
I have the windows open but you are so far away.
A breeze. Distant electricity. Skin.
We could talk on the phone but about what?
The weather?
Words have little to offer the hungry body —
how many ways can there be to say *want*,
to say *please*, to say *yes*,
to say *we sure could use some rain*?

Burn Ban

The redbuds — so much red
it's embarrassing.

The state issued a burn ban this morning—
something about dry air,
dead leaves,
wind.

We have canceled our afternoon plans — so much for that
cookout in a field of straw.
What a picnic it would have been!
How much of the landscape our love would have consumed!

An Experience I Have Not Had

is being called the wrong name during sex,

aloud. I think perhaps
I would not mind it. A glimpse

into some private yearning, an offer
to imagine my body as someone else's,

my own pleasure in skin
not my own. Who knows

what shape the language of desire
takes when it hits the air, like raindrops

that harden to pebbles of ice
upon contact with snowflakes

tumbling through the chilled surface
of our atmosphere. I don't remember

the word for this yet certainly I would
weep with joy if I heard it on your tongue.

The World We Live in Now

A rich man's vanity rocket explodes &
rains poison over a dozen neighborhoods & the sea
& this is just, like, Monday or whatever.
It's snowing where it shouldn't be snowing & at least
the snow might slow the fires. My father
texts to say they're all fine, don't worry
& I don't know if he means from a shooting
or a tornado or the zombie fungus
from that game they made into a TV show.
All the narratives we thought were cautionary tales
turn out to be blueprints. I thought at least
we'd agreed on who the assholes are in *Star Wars*,
but no, not even that.

Why Is One Side of a V of Birds Always Longer? It Has More Birds in It.

Saturday & cold sunshine & a crooked checkmark of Canada geese veers low overhead noisily. They bark & glide & shape themselves: river, rope bridge, narrative arc. The goose at the foremost point — would that be crisis? climax? crossroads? whatever, the bird wearies, its turn as leader complete, slides back toward one of the ends: resolution? catalyst? It's hard to keep track. Stories begin, they end, they overlap like seasons. The last time you touched me, I jumped. Bit my tongue. The blood warm against my teeth.

Clumsy Metaphor

a glass dropped
on kitchen floor

swept into dustpan

assembled

into a human body
by a human body

this is how desire
this is how

my life spent
broken   spilled

how I bleed
at the edge of you

So Warm for November, in Bed with the Windows Open

What if rhyme & rain — what if wet —
your hand on me —

what if mouth —

what if slick & sentence —
sidewalk

& someone passing by —
the laughter & the leaves

& the hush we hush
we rush & slow

whisper & wish
what if words
what if skin

were a song

If I Were a Language

What shapes would your tongue make
learning me? What if a single word
meant *sky* & *kiss* & *stranger*? If another
meant both *touch* & *hush*?
What if every word of me — every one of them —
came from your body, what then?
What would you name me?

Waking in a House That Has Not Yet Burned

When I wake my dream turns to ash as I reach for it. Outside the world turns to ash as I reach for morning. The rivers dry. Lakes dry. The icecaps hurl themselves from their own cliffs. I have never felt so helpless or I have always felt so helpless. The house where I grew up is ash. The house my mother moved to after is ash. So much fire. I feel like I'm being dramatic to mention it. Crying wolf. Only we're killing the wolves by killing the forests. Chicken Little, then. All the old cautionary tales. In the dream we were not touching. The sky was not falling, it was burning. The dream was of you. I'm sure it was you.

It Was the Word *Wet*, Wasn't It?

—after my tweet about the Carpenters song "Rainy Days
and Mondays" was flagged for containing "sensitive content"

I get it.
I, too, gather the word *wet* in my skin.
&, yes, I also remain
in love with Karen Carpenter
far beyond anything I'm entitled to.
However,

Mondays are just another day
that finds you living in a different time zone
& the last time we kissed in any kind of serious way
it might have been a Monday, sure.
Say, July, north Florida,
one of those afternoons
when the air was hot & (yes) wet
& at some point we peeled ourselves off our car seats
& our mouths off each other
& got on with the business of not-kissing

which if you ask me takes up entirely too much of a life
which I think is what the song is about.
I think it's what all songs are about.

If I'm on My Knees

it usually means there's a mess needs cleaning
so not exactly prayer   unless begging

the cat to stop peeing in the corner of the office
counts as prayer   I'm not down here
for any fun reason either

unless it's a special occasion   not
that I wouldn't   or we wouldn't
but you know how life goes

there's always some spill or another

a broken plate   the dog
into the garbage again
mud tracked from the outside
world into our lives

but if you want me   love
if you need me
you know where to find me

so maybe a kind of prayer after all

Fragment

If, in a given moment, I am not being touched —
in that moment, I would swear to you it has been decades
since I was touched, indeed I have never been touched.

At the Bar

Just buzzy enough to say without thinking I use my mouth a lot
& I'm talking about writing poems & go-to metaphors
& you are kind enough to laugh before the words
calcify into a problem. Still,
my face goes hot. My poems
are full of mouths & fingers
& fingers in mouths & I do want to be tasted.
I want to set free the shame
that animals hot through my blood
& I want you to unlatch the trap
& suddenly I miss the days
when we all smoked in places like this
to give our mouths something
to do, our fingers — the scratch
& flick & flame of a cheap lighter
illuminating tiny spaces between us,
& we'd go home smelling of the night we'd had
in our clothes & our hair & though
we now claim to prefer the world this way,
odorless & poison-free,
let's be honest, there
was magic in the fires we lit back then,
even the bitterest smoke
a middle finger to our body's weaknesses,
a *fuck you* to mortality & a *thank you* to desire
& it's always been our mouths that keep us alive, always.

American Highway

We're driving. There are no trees. We're driving
through a desert that used to be a park,
used to be lake, swamp, hiding place.
We're on the run. It's like a movie.
We turn up the music to drown out
the sun-ravaged landscape. It does not work.
We try a new song. The wind picks up,
a hot wind under a white, white sun.
Tumbleweeds race us, win. So much
whiteness. Under us asphalt melts, soup
of burning tar & human regret. We are
burning now. Driving. Burning. It's too late.
We understand at last what this is:
one of those movies where we both die
at the end, which is all movies.

Ode to ~~Infidelity~~

it's only ever been you but jesus there are so many versions of me
climbing into this bed every night

they say people behaving extravagantly want to be caught
all I want is to be held

what are you looking for when you climb onto me
what late-night sounds wake you

is it too warm in here
is it me

I'm calling no one else's name
no one else is answering

all I want is you to look at me
tell me something true

about this life we've built
one slow rhyme after another

one small patient lie at a time
one warm-hot night at a time

tell me I'm right
about what it means to be touched

Nice

is what we say to each other when words fail —
nice. That was nice. This has been nice. Nice.
What percentage, do you suppose, of people,
upon the occasion of their 69th birthday,
celebrate with a 69? Surely each person
thusly intertwined believes
in that wet-hot moment that their play
on words, their particular entanglement
of pun & pleasure must be unique
on all the planet. Is it disappointing
when you're not the first to have an idea?
You're not even the only person
right now with your face buried
in the flesh of someone you love
or love enough, at least, to share
this brief time. We say it
after weddings & funerals: *that was*
a nice service. So unoriginal,
this fussing we do over love & death,
hunger & grief, but original's
not the point. Our bodies
were born for this. To crave
& end. When someone my age dies
after an illness I wonder
about the last time they had sex.
I wonder about grief that has time
to rise that way, slowly, the body
growing used to its inevitable end, not
acceptance or anything like that, no,
but understanding, maybe. I wonder
about their spouse, how it feels
to watch such loss approaching
like the world's slowest

most terrible train
& then when it does arrive
it tornadoes past with a roar
& rush & then even then
despite so much warning
you must stand there
as if at a suddenly emptied station
staring out at empty tracks
thinking, *I thought — I thought*
there was more time. I thought
we'd have more. What was it like,
the last time they touched,
this couple? In my imagined version
of their love, it's all gentle
& grieving, full of awareness
of the body's fragility but I hope
I'm wrong. I hope
it was sweaty & exhausting.
I hope it erased the world
for a moment. I hope it was
more like a first time than a last,
& here I guess I'm betraying
my own desire for feeling new,
for the sense that my body
is an island being discovered
by a shipwreck survivor
so eager for solid ground
& sustenance, so thirsty
for fresh water — I'm being
ridiculous but that's the point,
I want it to be ridiculous
the way it was when we
first broke the rules together,
caught up in the miracle
that is mouth & finger,

touch & twist & nothing exists
outside of these bodies,
this room, this slaking
until we can barely breathe,
until the only tense is present,
until we look at each other
in shyness at the abandon,
how we revealed
so much about ourselves
& now here we are,
uncovered, reaching
for language to share
but words fail, that's what
I've been trying to say,
so, darling, come, stand wordless
with me at this window
& let us hold each other
& gaze at the world,
the morning rising,
the day that can go on without us.

At the Hardware Store I Realize, As Usual

At the hardware store I realize, as usual,
I've forgotten to measure. I have no clue
what size screw I need to fix the shower door
or if it's even a screw I need. I mumble
the screw I need until I'm blushing,
driving home undone, job delayed to another day,
a disappointment to my family in ways small enough
they'd never say so aloud. I need a nap. I'm still
wearing a mask. We're at the point again
where most are, but not all. Either way
it's a statement. How did I get here?
The first hardware store I remember
looked like the hardware store in a movie
about a man who works at a hardware store—
that wouldn't be the point of the movie,
a detail to illustrate that our hero
is both ordinary & useful. Mundane
but manly. The skill with tools we see early
will pay off later. The barrels of nails. Chain
by the link, rope in every thickness. I fear I've made this
into a zombie movie, or *War of the Worlds*,
some kind of invasion from which our hero
must save—his family? Everyone?
I've raised the stakes beyond all reason.
That hardware store had a cooler of cold drinks
near the checkout line. It was labeled cold drinks.
I knew better than even to ask my father,
busy & broke, in the middle of some duty
more important than my desire. How much of my life
have I spent staring into such a case, convinced
all I've ever wanted or needed in this world
whispers my name behind cold glass
as I thirst & thirst? Grape. Orange.
7-Up. RC Cola. Cheerwine. Forgive me.

Love Poem

There's a song with your name in it
but I can't listen to it

with anyone else in the room.
You slide your fingers

into my mouth & pull out
another word for this lake

we've made of our lives.
Each summer it goes drought-dry:

cracked field of mud,
surface of a strange planet.

What is left to say
about such distance?

What to say about rain
that our bodies don't already know?

Ledge (ars poetica) (love poem) (true story)

When I say ledge you immediately think of falling but it's the opposite a ledge is a thing we build into the emptiness so we have a place to stand. Of course it's dangerous risk of death & all that what do you think being alive involves. When I say step out onto this ledge with me does it sound like I'm talking about love or do you immediately go to the implied leap after. Wait until you find out a bridge is where two ledges meet halfway. Why are you always on about the abyss. No a river isn't any better have you ever landed on water the wrong way. You do have to watch your step it's true. There's room for us here for now & now is enough let us fit our bodies together let us balance our weight against each other let us hold on even as a hot wind rises.

Estuary, Delta, Confluence, Mouth

The water from a river can enter the receiving
body in a variety of different ways. — Wikipedia

O what I would give for you to ask me to start a fire
in our laundry room. One look & I'd be on my knees
digging for matches in a bottom drawer where maybe
we've hidden the evidence that once upon a time
we'd smoke together after the kids went to bed,
on the front porch during a summer rainstorm,
breathing in a little taste of shared mortality,
water misting through the screen against our innocent faces,
our little one-way street a river carrying the season
away from us, carrying one evening toward the next,
carrying our bodies through the days of our lives.
At the end of the street there's a drain. If we
sit here without speaking, if we listen & listen,
we can hear water disappearing. A sweet song.
I was saying recently how much I love
small rivers, how many small rivers
were in my life growing up, how each spring our yard
was a river. There was a fire, too, that licked
the dry straw of a fallow field & threatened
everything we had built. Maybe this is why
I spend my days in such a hurry — why I want
so much, why when I look at you in this flickering light
my hunger rises like smoke from my lips —
you'd think ambition would be fire, but water, too,
consumes & covers & drags away
what it cannot destroy. To be washed
clean & new — or to burn hot — what does it say
about me that I can't decide whether my fantasies
are flood or flame — whether I want to live in the river
or the place at the end where the river finds its home.

I'm Not Hungry but My Mouth Is Bored (distance) (marriage)

which direction are you from here
kidding I know it's down

I would be a better river than lake
wretched weary of waiting to be traveled to

my darling westward witch
my east my Eden my every

each of us one single individual water
amid all the many waters

nostalgic for spring & source
before we bend around the first bend

(facing the audience) you know
how long this took us

you think it's easy to meander
for a thousand years

in a ditch made by melting ice
(back to you) join me

the rocks are slippery
the cold takes the breath

I Am Pretty Sure My Neighbor Has Taken a Lover

I envy —
not the sex (not only the sex)

but the secret that fuels the sex.
The sharedness of it, the two of them

alone in their knowing
what it is to lay this singular specific body

atop this one other body. How common
the thirst, how specific

the slaking. My neighbor parks on the street,
leaves the garage open,

the lover pulls in, the door closes its mouth behind them
as I recall how you and I

started like that: lips open, breaking
a promise made to someone else,

fairy tale protagonists
lost in the dark wet woods

long before anyone knew
we were gone.

That gif You Send Me from That Show We Like

two silent seconds of wink & come-hither
that makes me believe in love & touch & holy
makes me believe we might make it

we might last   we might fall
happily into bed   stay for years
makes me believe we (species /

you & me) might be   at last
capable of being honest about desire
(maybe it's the wordlessness)

though we so rarely are I don't

remember the episode it's from
but I know how my skin peals
when you blink just blink in my direction

one body a bell   the other the sky awaiting music

Love Poem I Guess

You get inside me & hollow me out like a virus. I am left empty exhausted etc. God, it's exactly what I wanted. Now I can hear the wind testing the edges of the building; it sounds cold. You know what I mean. Claim my body, go ahead. Name it a gift, unwrapped as it is. We both know my desire is metaphor, is fantasy, there is no literal, you're not even here. Look, I am trying to provide you with a definition of pleasure. It has something to do with how long I can lie on my back without blankets. How long without curling into myself. How long your ghost lingers in this room. The chill of not being touched. Like frost unlacing from the surface of the planet in the face of a slow-arriving day.

Up Early, Three Months After Moving to a New State

Walking the dog before sunrise & there are so many stars over Ohio & I'm pretty sure that big one is Jupiter & Orion's Belt is so bright & I lift my eyes & lift my eyes & reach for the profound & which of course escapes into the dark spaces & between the sky & distance & distance & everyone is so far away & here I think I am supposed to & say how insignificant it all makes me feel & but it's the opposite & I am the center of the motherfucking universe & the hunter watches me & specifically me & it sounds like I'm talking about God & I'm not & I'm talking about & I sleep less here & I am lonely & I'm talking about & you & despite the stars & because of the stars.

Sex on the Beach

In a nation at war — but of course
nation means *at war* — we

turn to each other for solace.
Let turmoil

turmoil. Let us name
our own bodies.

Let us decide on the manner
of their joining.

& in this way,
in this act

of reaching
for what we want,

of naming our pleasure
after ourselves,

here,
naked,

in the cool sand
of an evening by water

let us save the whole entire goddamn world.

Garfield Minus Garfield

It has become a thing that every so often in America the romantic texts & emails between two inappropriately involved people become public in the wake of a scandal. Without fail they are humiliating to read, the worst kind of obituary for a love affair. Someone else's hunger matters only if there's at least the possibility it's directed at you. In the absence of actual desire, our attempts to express desire are banal as a dry sink in an empty apartment behind a dying mall in a Midwestern suburb that used to be a field where pheasants nested. If you remove the cat from the comic strip about the cat, the result is nihilism: a sad man talking to himself about death. If you remove the moon from a love poem, is it now an elegy? Or, it was elegy from the start.

Great / Salt / Lake

all this time / I've never asked / what your novel / is called /
she says / *Great Salt Lake* / I say / what's it about / she says /
two people in / love at the end / of the world / is it about us /
you / can / decide / the oceans / are / almost dry / the world is
/ a field of salt / how to build / a life / like this / the world / is
the taste of sweat / on your skin / we're / running out of time
/ that was always true / we / are already / undressed / your
thumb / in my mouth / will / save us

How Much Time Do We Have?

we stand at the edge of something unsayable /

sunlight against the surface of a lake /

I will undress in front of you but I am waiting for you to ask /

all the urgency of water /

cold of late afternoon /

at this point it's going to take a miracle /

that was always true /

what dazzles more than a body /

what is more green than shadow /

chorus of birds /

twilit days of our twilight love affair /

lifelong camping trip /

what is such a day if not miracle /

mountains in the distance /

always mountains /

always distance

What We're Leaving Behind (map)

dry lakebed & hot wind where music used to live

      dry lakebed & hot wind where bees used to
          dry lakebed & hot wound where the moon

      dry lakebed & no forest all dust
    dry lakebed & weed-cracked highways
        dry lakebed & what passed for love

            dry lakebed & empty
     dry lakebed & whatever follows regret in the dictionary
dry lakebed & creaking oil pumps in perpetual motion
     dry lakebed & out of gas anyway
           dry lakebed & hungry

         dry lakebed & ocean plastic
   dry lakebed & disposable diapers
dry lakebed & bleached cattle bones
       dry lakebed & what else did you expect
        dry lakebed & abandoned cars
    dry lakebed & what I promise was love
      dry lakebed & what comes after tree
        dry lakebed & it's all so obvious now
     dry lakebed & what comes after what comes
dry lakebed & our last drops of faith in metaphor evaporating
    dry lakebed & what   we can get used to
  dry lakebed & our plans to run away together
    dry lakebed & thirsty
      dry lakebed &   another dry lakebed

& so many empty rivers don't get me started on the rivers
            so many   so empty

Prayer with Burning Barn

My favorite barn burned down today.
I loved it for its imperfections,
its usedness, the way it sagged
against itself. Postcard red
worn to gray. Today
as I drove by, flame
bit the spring sky.
A plume of smoke
visible for a mile.
A line of flashing lights,
traffic narrowed to a single lane,
hoses containing the heat
but stopping nothing.
Tomorrow's commute
will offer a touch less
wonder. There's a hole
in my future shaped
like an old barn.
I do not mean
to make more of this
than what it is:
a story about the body.

Broken Sonnet with Climate Change & Office Hours

My student is writing an essay on climate change.
It's lovely but also pretty bleak, to be honest.

I say as I read the draft, "Yeah, we're probably screwed."
She says, "There's no *probably* about it."

I say, "I guess you're more screwed than I am."
She says, "Right, at least you won't be around for the end of it."

She means this as a kindness.
We laugh a little

& fall quiet
&, eventually,

return to the essay:
temporary respite in her words,

the hopes we share for them.

Invocation

we kept waiting for permission to begin
first ask grace or whatever

drove south around the big lake

slept together in someone else's bed
frumpy floral overstuffed comforter

slow rattle & shadow of an old ceiling fan
humid skin hungry skin
we posed in the background of each other's photos

ate each other's laughter & felt full
we stepped into the cold black water

so long ago & yet still I taste the sand on our lips

we prayed for forgiveness
in case we didn't get away with it but we did

we did

Ode to the Oceans' Many Plastic Patches

disappointing-ass way to kill the planet if you ask me
no music in it at all
what if instead convenience
wasn't god

when I was eleven I joined the world
learned all the wrong lessons
about what matters

still unlearning
(not really)

mostly my problems have to do with hunger
mostly my problems have to do

I don't litter
haven't littered
in years but there was a brief period

when I bought cigarettes on my way home from work
did not smoke them
threw the pack out the window mistaking

this for freedom

I guess I got away with it

anyway the idea of these plastic patches
it's fucking terrible
shittiest detritus of the shittiest century

look the numbers are too big for a body to hold
gyre of waste three times the size of France
how big can France even be

I did learn to slice the rings from a six-pack
still do
for the seals, you know
mistake is thinking we can save anything

such pleasure in not smoking
only if you have the cigarettes in your hand first

don't mean to sound hopeless
don't know how else to end this
don't know how else it ends

Twenty Minutes to Save the World GO

A man comes up to me says you have twenty minutes to save
the world won't tell me what it needs saving from apparently
supposed to be obvious red wire or blue pick one something
along those lines stop using fossil fuels nope too late for that
one HA HA this man is a little fellow with a mustache a
dumb hat he's pissing me off can I make a phone call what do
you think this is a game show what do you think you're being
arrested no phone call your time is almost up you said twenty
minutes apparently he lied it's time it's time it's time I wasted
so much time thinking how I would tell you about this later
we would laugh about the hat we would laugh OH how we
would have laughed

Ode to the Bees (the bees can stay)

How to talk about my life (or bees) without the word *busy*?
     An hour is whatever
  it is, what difference how we spend it? Rain doesn't

    think itself busy as it falls. A daffodil
 busy for existing as a daffodil, all petal & pollen

 & beautiful mouth open to the world? No.

To spend a day looking for lilacs to photograph —

    that would feel not busy. To do no harm —

or at least no more. To wake late, bedroom already sundrenched,
    headachy from last night's buzziness.

To roll over & see you still here, waking in the same instant,
  to kiss
     away the sour breath of mourning.

   To take the day slow. To move less. To rescue
nothing, to save the saving for another time.
    But what if

  there is no more time, no next day?
     All the more reason.
The moon never stops moving — stupid lovely moon —

   yet no poet celebrates the moon
    merely for its industriousness.

We are wrong about the moon. We have been wrong
   about almost everything, all our lives. Knowing ourselves

unworthy of salvation doesn't make us worthy. And yet —
already time slips away. We must go.

The bees? If it's not too much to ask. The bees can stay.

ACKNOWLEDGMENTS

I do not write alone. For me, poetry exists in and because of community.

Thank you, thank you, thank you to my family—Ellen, Zoe-Kate, and Eli—for always supporting me. I could not do any of this without you.

Thank you to Han VanderHart for being my partner at River River Books and for reading this book before it was a book. Thank you to Jen Stein and Brandon Amico for feedback on early versions of the manuscript. Thank you to Maggie Smith and Erin Elizbeth Smith whose past editorial feedback taught me so much about putting together a collection of poems. Thank you to Chis Haven, Adam Schuitema, and Pablo Peschiera for the Friday mornings at Schuler. Thank you to my pal and collaborator W. Todd Kaneko. Thank you to Dean Rader, Christina Olson, Brian Komei Dempster, Jean Prokott, Judy Halebsky, Brian Clements, and the rest of the Poet's Choice gang past and present for leading me to many of the poems in this book. Thank you to my students for keeping me on my toes. Thank you to to Stephannie Gearhart and Chad Van Buskirk for laughs and love during a time of transition, and thank you to all my colleagues at both Grand Valley State and Bowling Green State for your support and motivation.

Thank you to Erin Schmerr for the brilliant cover image (and to Sara Moore Wagner for connecting us), and to Allison Lange for the cover design.

Thank you to Sandra Beasley, Molly Spencer, and Steven Leyva.

Thank you to Dr. Ross Tangedal and the editors on the Cornerstone team for ushering this book into the world with care and attention.

And of course thank you so much to the editors of the journals where many of these poems first appeared, sometimes in different form or under different title:

- *American Poetry Review*: So Warm for November, in Bed with the Windows Open
- *Asterales*: I Am Pretty Sure My Neighbor Has Taken a Lover
- *Black Lily Zine:* Ode to the Bees (the bees can stay)
- *Defunct Magazine*: At the Hardware Store I Realize, As Usual
- *diode poetry journal*: Estuary, Delta, Confluence, Mouth
- *DMQ Review*: Up Early, Three Months After Moving to a New State and Why Is One Side of a V of Birds Always Longer? It Has More Birds in It.
- *HAD*: Broken Sonnet with Climate Change & Office Hours
- *Identity Theory*: The Phrase Is "Comfortable in Your Own Skin" but Who Has Ever Felt Such a Thing?
- *Kissing Dynamite*: I Have Been Trying to Make Sense of Love Again
- *Midway Journal*: What We're Leaving Behind (map)
- *Moist Poetry Journal*: I'm Not Hungry but My Mouth Is Bored (distance) (marriage)
- *Moon City Review*: We Wake Each Day in This World We've Made Together
- *Nixes Mate*: Ode to the Seediest Motel in Kentucky
- *ONE ART*: Fragment
- *Only Poems*: Irreconcilable (ars poetica) (love poem); Clumsy Metaphor; Ode to the Oceans' Many Plastic Patches; Ode to My Stupid Mouth; For So Long, I Was Foolishly Proud of The Scar on My Thumb; Ode

to ~~Infidelity~~; Love Poem ("There's a song"); Nice

o *pacificREVIEW*: "It Was the Word Wet, Wasn't It?"
o *Postcard*: What the Moon Sees in Us
o *Psaltery & Lyre*: Ode to Temptation
o *Public School Poetry*: An Experience I Have Not Had; Dryer the Ground, More Dangerous the Floods; If I'm on My Knees
o *Rejection Letters*: Ode to the Moon (the moon is an unreliable narrator) (the river too)
o *Stone Circle Review*: If I Were a Language
o *Sontag Mag*: American Highway
o *The Boiler*: How Much Time Do We Have?
o *The Cincinnati Review*: Ledge (ars poetica) (love poem) (true story)
o *The Florida Review*: Prayer with Burning Barn
o *The London Magazine*: Garfield Minus Garfield
o *The Missouri Review*: Bodies, in Concert
o *The Prose Poem*: What Happens When a Star Explodes
o *Twelve Mile Review*: At the Bar
o *UCity Review*: Invocation
o *$ (Poetry Is Currency)*: Waking in a House That Has Not Yet Burned

An excerpt from "Bodies, in Concert" was featured on *The Slowdown Show* podcast. "For So Long, I Was Foolishly Proud of The Scar on My Thumb" and "At the Bar" were each reprinted at *Verse Daily*. "Ledge (ars poetica) (love poem) (true story)" was reprinted in *Best Small Fictions 2025* and featured on *The Slowdown Show*. "Waking in a House That Has Not Yet Burned" was inspired in part by Cameron Awkward-Rich's "Meditations in an Emergency." "Love Poem" ("My body") appears in the chapbook *Extinction Level* (Tram Editions, 2025).

AMORAK HUEY is author of four previous books of poetry, including *Dad Jokes from Late in the Patriarchy*. Co-founder with Han VanderHart of River River Books, Huey is director of the creative writing program at Bowling Green State University in Ohio. He is co-author with W. Todd Kaneko of the textbook *Poetry: A Writer's Guide and Anthology* and the chapbook *Slash/Slash*. Huey is a recipient of a fellowship from the National Endowment for the Arts, and his poems have appeared in *The Best American Poetry, American Poetry Review, The Southern Review,* and the Academy of American Poets' Poem-A-Day series.

www.ingramcontent.com/pod-product-compliance
Lightning Source LLC
Chambersburg PA
CBHW030501130626
46549CB00007B/2814

* 9 7 8 1 9 6 8 1 4 8 2 8 7 *